# Carrie Goes Farming

Written by Dexter Ashford
Illustrator by Nicole Reasonda
Edited by Samantha Sanabia
Book Design by Rosemarie Gillen



FIRST EDITION

Paperback ISBN: 979-8-89145-563-4

Printed in the U.S.A.

*To my daughter, Carrie Michelle.*
*Daddy loves you to no end.*

Written by **Dexter Ashford**
Edited by **Samantha Sanabia**
Illustrated by **Nicole Reasonda**

My name is Carrie,
And I'm a busy girl.
Here's Mom and Dad.
They're my whole world!

I am very excited.
Today is the day!
Let's go to the farm.
I've got a lot to say.

Let's plant a garden.
I'll teach you how.
So let's get ready.
Let's start now!

Step one is important.
Now let's not forget.
Let's make the soil
Into a nice pretty bed.

Our plants also need
A nice sunny spot.

They like the heat,
But I think it's too hot!

While Daddy works,
I like to play.
Running on the farm.
What a fun day!

But one thing I don't like,
They're just no fun,
Is a big ugly bug.
They make me run!

On the farm we can see
Many pretty things.
Brightly colored flowers
And birds that sing.

Red peppers,
Brown potatoes.
Juicy apples,
Sweet tomatoes.

Tomatoes, you say?
Those are the best!
Step two is to pick seeds
For our gardening quest.

Now that we know
What we want to start,
Here's step three
Of our work of art.

We put the seeds
Into the ground.
Cover them with dirt,
And they're safe and sound.

Step four is a chore
But important, you see.
Water your plants,
And they'll grow with glee!

When Dad is tired,
Mom jumps in.
She waters the plants.
And they give the sun a grin!

Now it's time to gather
With everyone.
Let's eat what we've grown,
And then we'll be done!

The food is amazing.
We can't fit one more bite.
Now Mom says it's time
To say, "Good night."

So there you have it.
Now you have learned
How to plant a garden.
A break, you have earned.

But not just yet.
Can you recall?
Steps one through four.
Can you remember them all?

Step one is important.
Now let's not forget.
Let's make the soil
Into a nice pretty bed.

Step two is to pick seeds
For our gardening quest.

Here's step three
Of our work of art.

We put the seeds
Into the ground.
Cover them with dirt,
And they're safe and sound.

Step four is a chore
But important, you see.
Water your plants,
And they'll grow with glee!

We're at the end of our day.
What fun we have had...

I hope you'll come back for more
Of Carrie, Mom, and Dad!

Dexter Ashford lives in Columbia, SC with his wife, Connie, and their daughter, Carrie. Dexter earned both his BS and his MS degrees in Agribusiness from South Carolina State University.

He is the owner of Ashford Family Farms, LLC and the founder of The Urban Farming Project, a movement to teach people how to grow big food in small spaces.

He hosted the Urban Farming Project Conference in June of 2018 to share with his audience several concepts of urban growing and various uses of land plots both big and small. Mr. Ashford has also started a hydroponic grow house that can be used to produce fresh food year round. Additionally, he has hosted planting days for community organizations and has spoken to incarcerated youth about the importance of healthy food production in their communities. Mr. Ashford founded the Urban Farming Project Farmers Market, which ran from April to August and served primarily local food desert areas. He now teaches basic gardening skills in schools and community centers in his local area.

www.ingramcontent.com/pod-product-compliance
Ingram Content Group UK Ltd.
Pitfield, Milton Keynes, MK11 3LW, UK
UKHW060116300726
14090UKWH00002B/232

*9798891455634*